CORNELIUS M. PIETZNER **VILLAGE LIFE** THE CAMPHILL COMMUNITIES

Copyright © 1986 Cornelius M. Pietzner
Published by Neugebauer Press, Salzburg–Munich–London–Boston.
Distributed in USA by Alphabet Press, Natick, MA.
Distributed in Canada by Vanwell Publishing, St. Catharines.
Distributed in U.K. by Ragged Bears, Andover.
Distributed in West Germany by Neugebauer Press, Munich.
All rights reserved.
Printed in Austria.

LIBRARY OF CONGRESS CATALOGING IN PUBLICATION DATA

Village Life.

1. Camphill Movement. 2. Mentally handicapped—United States.
3. Mentally handicapped—United States—Pictorial works.
I. Pietzner, Cornelius M. II. Pietzner, Carlo, 1915-1986. III. Root, Wanda.
HV3006.A4V54   1986   362.3'85   86-12716
ISBN 0-88708-030-8

VILLAGE LIFE

THE CAMPHILL COMMUNITIES

edited by Cornelius M. Pietzner
forward by Pete Seeger
essays by Carlo Pietzner & Wanda Root
poem by Martin Sheen
photographs by Charles Carlson III,
Cornelius M. Pietzner,
Stephan Rasch

NEUGEBAUER PRESS

TABLE OF CONTENTS

FORWARD

There once was a time when people were gentle. Perhaps instead of writing a forward, I should be writing a backward. In any case, looking at these pictures, we can agree: there should be more places like the Camphill communities.
How to "get" them? Impossible. We can only build them, inch by inch, in our lives, in our hearts. But we can learn, and this book will help.
One of the big advantages of books over the television medium is that one can stop at a page and think about it. One can turn back and get new meaning from a picture or paragraph that one skipped by quickly at the first reading. And looking at the face of one individual we can then start thinking of other individuals and our mind has taken off on a flight.
One caution: our words may mislead us. No word I know but can be stretched by a poetic mind, and its borders disagreed upon. Therefore, let us keep a sense of humor, even though we are talking about such things as life and death, not just for individuals, but of all humanity, of all of this oasis in space, this planet Earth.
An insignificant dot. Our home.

Pete Seeger

DEDICATION

While this book was being produced

CARLO PIETZNER

passed away on April 17, 1986. He was a co-founder of the Camphill Movement, and pioneered the work in the United States.
VILLAGE LIFE is dedicated to him in gratitude for his manifold contributions, and in celebration of 25 years of activity in America.

EDITOR'S REMARKS

The thought of giving visual expression to an amazingly rich and multifaceted way of life represents an exciting challenge. To photographically depict a few of the principles which permeate this village life heightens the challenge. Our book is an attempt to convey and share some ideas about a particular kind of village life. It is not only a documentary project. It is also not a book just about handicapped people. It is a book about people trying to consciously live together in new ways by creating their own environment as far as possible. It is about a creative social effort which includes mentally handicapped children and adults in the Camphill village communities.

The concept of integrated, intentional communities like Camphill presents a unique opportunity to a publication which tries to avoid mere reportage. We have attempted to illustrate some important aspects of these villages and to share images which would provide accurate visual evidence of Camphill life. Some of these images, which show festival celebrations, the social interdependence of people, and the dignity of work and play, are readily identifiable. Others must be seen in combination, and against the ever-changing social backdrop of a partially self-sufficient village.

Each Camphill community has its own special characteristics, yet common elements can be recognized. How could one capture these elements without being repetitive? This was not just an organizational or technical question, but required us to be as clear and objective as possible about what those common principles were and how they manifest themselves in each village community.

It has been a challenge to select representative images of life in the communities. There are far more than can be included here. This editorial question is enhanced when one understands that a potent element in the community fabric is the attempt to uplift and transform the ordinary relationships of everyday life. Thus the photography can only depict the outcome or visible expression of what is an ongoing and largely intangible process.

To some extent the book contains sections marked by the change from black and white to color photography. The initial pictures show architectural portraits, usually the community centers, or halls. The implied question of what happens in these buildings, what they are for, is answered in the main body of the book, and illustrated towards the end through the cultural events and by the festival celebrations which are so important to Camphill life.

One may notice also that the portrait section in the middle, which forms the bridge between the school, or children's village, and the villages for adults, serves as a fulcrum to the balance of the book. It is people who form the villages, and it is around these people that school takes place — the first part of the book — and the work and social life of the adult village occurs — the second part of the book.

The sequencing is gentle; there are no formal chapter breaks. The school grades ascend from the youngest up to the older children, who are already involved in land work and other activities.

This rhythm is repeated in the portraits in a general way, and leads to subtle progressions in the latter sections. For instance, one can notice pictures of animal care, and hay and fodder storing, chicken feeding (eggs), the bakery — where bread and rolls are made — then served, maybe even with maple syrup. In this manner one can perhaps sense the flow of daily life and the correlation between one village activity and another.

We hope the photographs can encourage an inner experience for the viewer. One may notice, at least visually, that the parameters of normality and abnormality become arbitrary. In an age of convenience and classification it is only too easy to find restricting labels for highly complex, subtle, and mysterious phenomena in people. Through these images our book tries to break through the segregation of classification.

If one examines the portraits one can ask: "Is that person handicapped or not?" If one looks even more intently one might sense: "This countenance expresses outwardly what I sometimes feel inwardly. And when I have this feeling then this person would express me better than I could do myself!"

In fact, if we are honest with ourselves, we can sometimes notice that we exhibit tendencies that the handicapped person simply expresses to a greater extent. Thus by experiencing and depicting human beings of all kinds living and working together with purpose, one can perhaps sense that a handicap is an added quality, not a final specification or label.

This is yet another aim of these photographs. If individually and collectively, the images can stimulate such thoughts, private as they may be, about the social and spiritual texture of diverse people contributing together to community life, the effort will have been justified.

The results of this project have been considerably enhanced by the help and advice of a number of people. I would like to express gratitude to all of those within Camphill who helped guide the book's development and allowed the photographers various intrusions into their lives and work over a period of fifteen months. Some of these must be singled out.

Andrew Hoy has been like a gentle wind to fill the sails since the beginning. His vision and perseverance helped keep the project alive and in proper perspective. The momentum he provided was invaluable. Clemens Pietzner worked substantially to facilitate support through the Camphill Foundation, and helped in any way he could.

Without question, this whole effort has been refined through the support and collaboration of Michael Neugebauer of Neugebauer Press. One could ask for no more in a publisher. His comments and advice have been artistic and precise; without him there would be no book.

Others also have actively participated in this effort. William Herman, Carrie Riley, and George Kalmar provided resources and photographs, while various individuals gave advice and encouragment.

I would like to state my personal gratitude and thanks in working with photographers Stephan Rasch, Charles Carlson and Michael Leonard. Both Mr. Rasch and Mr. Leonard made an enormous effort to produce the final prints for publication with an unforgiving deadline. Throughout the planning and execution of this book, through much correspondence and many meetings, the enthusiasm and commitment of each photographer carried the project during the thin months. One can only be grateful to each for what they have given, despite full-time responsibilities elsewhere. This has been a cooperative experience; without them the book could not exist.

Lastly I would like to thank all those who appear within these pages, and the many who do not, but constitute so centrally the Camphill Community. Without the special children and the adult "villagers" who provide so much depth and meaning, enriching and fructifying village life, none of what this book attempts to portray would exist. These are truly exceptional individuals and their contribution to village life cannot be overestimated. In so many unexpected and delicate ways, they are the teachers and they are the counselors and the mediators.

This publication is not intended as a conclusive statement on Camphill in North America. Rather it is an attempt at giving expression to some of the diverse aspects of village life in these communities. Such an effort can only be partial, as the essential human and social experience within the communities transcends pictorial representation. Nevertheless, as a contribution directed outside the communities, elements of Camphill village life may resonate in these pages.

Cornelius M. Pietzner

CAMPHILL VILLAGES · A WAY OF LIFE

There is a wooded, quiet valley in rural upstate New York. There are some old red barns, cows graze in the outlying meadows, and a brook runs through the valley. A peace-drenched, seemingly forgotten place, it is the home of Camphill Village. When you enter this Village-in-the-valley, you enter a certain timelessness.

In the heart of the Village, glowing red through the trees, stands a strikingly faceted, thoroughly modern building, Fountain Hall. Below it lies the Hall Pond, quietly reflecting the ever-changing Village life. In spring, this is the place to catch first signs of new life, squirming tadpoles and salamanders. In summer there are picnics, games, folkdancing, and cacaphonous bullfrog choruses. In autumn it gathers windblown russet leaves, and in winter it hums with skaters.

Fountain Hall is the gathering place for this Village community. Its vaulting interior hosts cultural, artistic, educational, and social activities. The Village assembles here to celebrate a festival, a wedding, a special birthday. Musical gifts are shared through concerts, choirs, and speech choruses which resound within its walls. Sometimes guest performers entertain. Plays, skits, and pageants are held, as well as meetings, lectures, and common study. The community gathers here for worship. Like rays from this center, footpaths reach through the woods, over the brook, past fields, across the road, uphill and down, leading to neighborhoods of houses, the old barn, the new farm complex, craftshops, co-op store and garden. Within this landscape over 200 people live together in an intentional therapeutic community. About half are mentally handicapped adults. Come, choose a path, walk down it and enter this landscape. How soon someone comes to meet you. Come, take a tour. Your guide greets you with an ear-reaching grin, an energetic and prolonged handshake, and bubbling vivacity. She seems proud that you have come to see her Village. The way she talks, you might think she owned the place. And in a way, she does.

Along the way, you pass a tall, determined, rather elegant man intently guiding a profoundly handicapped woman down the country road. Suddenly, he drops her hand, spins around three times, bends down, picks up a leaf, and crumbles it between his fingers. He sniffs it, gingerly, then goes back to fetch his charge and proceeds with renewed determination. You meet many people on their way to work, and they check your progress repeatedly. "Who are you?" "Nice day!" "You happy?" "It's my birthday tomorrow!" "You like it here?" There is openness, friendliness, and warmth.

Climb up the hill to the Birchtree workshops, a high, light, modern complex of three craftshops. First you go to the candle shop; such fragrant peace reigns there. Some workers carefully dip candles, others sit around a table polishing, trimming, or packing them. Then you come to the book bindery, an airy and calm shop full of quiet industry and concentration. People are cutting, folding, sewing, glueing. There is a pile of handmade books, covered in fabric woven or batiked in the Village. The enamel shop is next. The room is painted a bold fuchsia, and hanging plants bloom in the windows. Here sits our pirouetting friend, settled down to polish copper. Others are involved in the various stages of enamelling. The workmaster gets down from his bench to greet you. There are some finished products on display, bowls and platters with transparent, flowing colors and forms. What unexpected beauty!

"Come along," your guide suggests, "there's much more to see!"

You meet a baker along the road, who is still aproned and capped in white, carrying a bright blue bucket of fresh loaves. Someone else approaches, does not stop or even raise his head, but only continues on slowly, buried in solitude. An officious looking gentleman passes. He nods rather curtly, checks his timepiece, and moves right along with his attaché case under his arm. An inspector? No, he is the Village courier, delivering internal mail and messages. Do you hear that loud "Ya-a-Hoo-o-!" echoing down the valley? The farmers are bringing the cows in from pasture. One farmer wears an unusual three-cornered hat — his T-shirt — wrapped around his head. The other has a broad, contagious grin. If you follow their footsteps, you would come to Sunny Valley barn where you could watch them feed and hand-milk their cows.

Here come the gardeners; their wheelbarrows overflow with spinach and onions. One stops, picks up a basket of vegetables and carries it to a house. He wipes his muddy boots, hastily, and proceeds through the bootroom inside. Would you like to go inside too?

You wander into the living-dining room. There is a round wooden table set for 12 with a vase of fresh flowers in the center on a hand-woven cloth. The windowsills are filled with plants and crystals. Original artworks adorn the walls. Your guide pops into the kitchen. "Hi", she says. "How was my soup this morning? Did you like it? What are you making for supper?" And then to you: "I work here in the mornings and today I made borscht. Here is my workmaster." You meet the housemother with a crew of helpers. They might be preparing supper, making jam, shaking cream into butter, or beginning to process the newly delivered basketful of vegetables. Someone may be cleaning out closets, ironing, or mending.

"Well," your guide says, "I've got to go back to my work-place. They need me now. It was a pleasure to meet you."

If you had really taken a tour of the Village, your guide would have made sure you had also seen the woodshop, the dollshop, the bakery, the weaving shop, and the garden. You would have been reminded to stop at the gift shop on your way out of the Village. Indeed, you would have been invited into a Village house, where you would have been received by a housemother, offered refreshments and the opportunity to ask some of your questions. "What is this place, what is Camphill?" "What are you doing?" "How do you do it?" "For whom?" "Why?"

Camphill is an impulse for social renewal through community living. This impulse is inspired by Anthroposophy, the world view of the Austrian philosopher, scientist, and educator, Rudolf Steiner, Ph.D. (1861-1925). Anthroposophy might be described as a path to understanding man in his relationship with the physical and spiritual world. It is a pursuit of the meaning of existence. In its practical application, Anthroposophy has inspired new directions in fields as varied as the arts, the sciences, religion, medicine, education, special education, architecture, pharmacology, and agriculture.

In 1937 in Vienna, a number of medical students, artists, and educators came together in search of an ideal. They formed a group to study Anthroposophy, and were led by Karl König, an eminent Viennese pediatrician and the former medical superintendent of a large residential special school in Germany. He was a man of courage, enormous compassion, and vision. In 1938, under Dr. König's leadership, this group decided to undertake a common task. Camphill owes its existence largely to his deep humanity from which innovative therapeutic and social insights arose.

The work of Camphill began in 1939, just before the outbreak of World War II, when members of the group, now refugees from Middle Europe, gathered in a stone manse in the northeast of Scotland. In the midst of strife and chaos, and the dissolution of social forms and values, they wanted to create a new form of social life. They wanted to find a way to live together based on a new understanding of man, and the ideals of freedom, equality, and brotherhood. They intended to create a healing environment, a therapeutic community in which to care for and share life with children in need of special care.

The first children came to join them. Life was full of work and discovery. The needs of the children helped create the forms of life. There were common meals, common work, common joys and common sorrows, common study, and common striving. Home life, school life, and therapeutic activities grew and developed. "Curative Education", Rudolf Steiner's new direction in the field of special education, took root within the Camphill community context. Soon other schools were established to meet the ever-growing demand. The children also grew, and a new challenge was posed: Could Camphill create a therapeutic community with mentally handicapped adults? New forms and approaches were needed. In time the Village concept was born, and Camphill ventured into the field of Social Therapy.

From these modest beginnings the movement grew. Parents and friends in other countries learned about Camphill and through their interest and initiative the work gradually expanded. There are presently 70 Camphill communities, specializing in Curative Education and Social Therapy, located in Northern and Middle Europe, Great Britain, Ireland, Africa, South America, and the United States. The movement is comprised of autonomous yet affiliated therapeutic community endeavors. Each is varied in size, scope, orientation, and character, depending upon the specific strengths and needs of the individuals living together, and the surrounding natural and cultural environments.

The variety of Camphill communities is substantial: a small agricultural Village in an old silk factory in the south of France; a few "council houses" in a planned urban development in the outskirts of London; a bustling Village of more than 300 people in the Yorkshire moors of England, comprised of five farms, a school, four stores, a post office, a printing press, and many craftshops. A school in Botswana offers a training program for native teachers and mothers of handicapped children in which they acquire the skills necessary to care for their children in their own native settlements. Twenty-five pioneers farm the land in Minnesota, establishing a new Camphill Village.

Not only is the movement international in scope, but each center is international in flavor as well. Co-workers come together from all parts of the world. This offers a rich cultural exchange and lends variety to each setting. Young people often travel from country to country via Camphill, participating in a movement-wide training course. An experienced co-worker might leave a settled community in Wales, for example, to help establish or support a younger venture in Austria.

The work of Camphill has gained recognition within the professional field. Its centers are approved and licensed as required. Villages have received awards and citations for merit and excellence. They host conferences of doctors, social workers, psychiatrists, and educators. Increasingly, Camphill is asked to participate in exhibitions, workshops, panels, and conferences in the professional field of mental retardation, as well as in crafts, education, agriculture, and the arts.

Beyond individual differences, there are certain characteristics that all Camphill communities share. The fundamental task in each setting is the same: to recognize and uphold that beyond the limitations of physical or mental disability there is in each individual an intact, inviolable, spiritual integrity. Each community attempts to order life in a threefold way, working toward a harmonious interplay of activity within the areas of social, cultural, and economic life.

Within each center, life is shared by people with and without mental handicaps in an integrated residential community setting. Each Village is comprised of individual households in which children, trainees, or adult "Villagers" with mental handicaps live together with "co-workers" and their children. These family settings create social warmth and security, which provide a basis for mutual understanding as well as individual guidance. These extended families share all the joys, sorrows, and intimacies of home life. This is home for all who live here.

Three times every day all members of a house community gather for meals. These are important social events. Where have the "family members" been between breakfast and lunch? Wait, you will hear. But first, a common grace will be spoken or sung. Now comes the chance for lively exchange. "My warp was finished this morning. I started weaving a blanket." "Someone's sick down at Bungalow," reports a Village gossip. "Did you hear what came up in the Administration meeting?" "Buh pee, buh pee, buh pee." "Michael wants the butter," says his solicitous neighbor, "Please wake up and pass it to him." "How did the play rehearsal go?" "A new calf was born this morning. Yep, Daisy had one, she did!"

Social interaction takes on an entirely new dimension within the context of Camphill community life. Life is shared with people from diverse social and cultural backgrounds and varied ages, with a wide range of capacities as well as limitations: a challenge and an ongoing education. This diversity of life brings social enrichment! How often the strength of one person balances the weakness of another. Through the unexpected interrelationships which develop, mutual help becomes a therapeutic reality. The faithfulness of a slow, methodical individual can calm the restlessness of a hyperactive, oversensitive soul. The warmth and generosity of a Down's Syndrome child can inhibit the isolation of another. A new co-worker can be roused out of self-absorption by the stirring needs of a severely handicapped child.

This sharing of life is deepened through religious observances. There is a weekly Bible Evening everywhere in Camphill. If you stepped into the dining room on a Saturday evening you would experience a different kind of meal, and a different quality of conversation. The Bible Evening is a preparation for the Christian services that take place each Sunday.

A striking characteristic of Camphill communities is the rich, active, and varied cultural life, which is created largely by and with handicapped people. A Village creates much of its own entertainment, calling on the creativity, initiative, goodwill, and enthusiasm of many. There are diverse opportunities for participation, such as an orchestra, a choir, or drama groups. Some people may folkdance, while others might join in eurythmy, a new art of movement devised by Rudolf Steiner.

Education is an ongoing concern. Each center offers opportunities for continuing education, growth, and development, commensurate to the needs of the people in its care. Formal 3–4 year in-service training courses in Curative Education and Social Therapy are offered for co-workers in centers throughout the movement. These courses complement the daily experience of Village life through common study, theoretical courses, and artistic activities.

Village life is enriched by a sense of occasion. The days, weeks, and changing seasons are acknowledged and highlighted. And how many special moments there are! There is always something to celebrate. A special song may mark the turn to autumn; the first furrow might be plowed in spring with the whole Village in attendance. The end-of-term may occasion a school festival with a play and music, or the end of the work week may be marked with an impromptu concert. A 70th birthday could inspire a call for a "Mayor of the Village" award complete with installation ceremonies. A song, poem, or prayer might accompany the evening hours.

The days, weeks, and seasons are imbued with celebration which culminates in the observance of the Christian festivals. Village life gains form and substance through engaging the whole community to prepare for the celebration of a festival. These celebrations are fundamental to the existence of community life.

There are many areas of work and opportunity in Camphill. Whether one is administrating in the office, weeding in the garden, teaching in the classroom, or peeling potatoes in the kitchen, all work is voluntary and based on mutual recognition, shared responsibility, and brotherly interdependence. Homemaking is considered a high priority. There is an art to serving a meal well, to placing a dozen people appropriately around the table, to creating an atmosphere of beauty and harmony. There is also an art to maintaining the home and to "running a household" in such a way that it becomes a source of security and really feels like "home" for all its diverse family members. Houseparents, children, Villagers, and working crews all help to bring about the creation of a house community. Work on the land is also important. Farms, gardens, orchards, woodlands, and grounds are maintained and cultivated by working crews. Members of the "estate crew", for example, perform tasks which vary with the seasons. They are out with rakes and wheelbarrows in autumn to gather up the leaves. They shovel snow and cut wood in winter. In early spring they tap maple trees, hang buckets, gather sap, and make syrup. The estate crew joins the farmers for haymaking each summer. Landwork provides meat, eggs, milk, cheese, vegetables, fruits, grains, and firewood. Craftwork is another ingredient of Village life. Trainees and Villagers who work in various craftshops produce items of beauty and utility. The emphasis in these shops is on quality and the processes and techniques of the crafts themselves, which require skill, patience, and diligence. In the weaving shop, for example, work may begin with raw wool shorn from Village sheep. In autumn the weavers might harvest berries to make natural dyes. Next they card and spin the wool and warp the loom. Then the weaving commences. Some of the Villagers are members of a weavers' guild and have had their work exhibited. Other craft activities include spinning, batiking, enamelling, bookbinding, doll-making, pottery, woodworking, and candlemaking.

Within the broad context of therapeutic community life, three specific therapeutic environments have been developed to meet the different needs of the child, adolescent, and adult with mental handicaps and special social needs. These environments may be found in the North American region of the Camphill movement, in the Villages of Beaver Run, Triform, and Kimberton Hills. Camphill Special Schools, Beaver Run is located on gently rolling, Pennsylvania farmland. It is a children's Village. It is a home for Curative Education. What does this mean? Imagine for a moment that you are walking up the hill in Beaver Run, past clusters of unusual, beautiful houses, up toward Rainbow Hall, the community center, and the Karl König Schoolhouse. Step into a house, just for a moment. There you meet the house community, half of whom are mentally handicapped children, and the others, co-workers and their families. Some of the co-workers are houseparents, or teachers, therapists, nurses, the doctor, the gardener, eurythmists, craftsmen, administrators, or some combination thereof. Others are dormitory parents who look after the daily needs of the children and also take the four-year training course in Curative Education.

13

The school bell rings. From all around the Village, the children stream toward the schoolhouse. Some run alone, others are accompanied by a co-worker. A few wear helmets to buffet epileptic falls. Others are kept well in hand in order to safely reach their destination. If you met them on the school-house steps, what a welcome you'd receive! Someone would want to know your name and where you came from. Others would eagerly wait their turn to shower you with attention. Another would be glad to take your hand, just for a moment. A bolder child might claim that hand and lead you into the schoolhouse.

Karl König House is a color-filled and harmonious "children's house of learning." The classrooms are light and beautiful. Here the mentally handicapped children participate in a comprehensive program based on a curriculum developed by Rudolf Steiner for the Waldorf Schools. This approach empha-sizes the social, artistic, and practical capacities as well as cognitive development. It addresses the whole child: head, heart, and limbs. Principle lessons are taught in intensive blocks of 3–6 week courses in subjects such as history, geography, mythology, sciences, as well as in reading, writing, and arithmetic. Artistic work is used to heighten the understanding of these subjects. Painting, drama, speech, poetry, singing, eurythmy, modelling, handwork, recorder playing, woodwork, are all part of the curriculum. The children are actively engaged in learning. A child allowed to play David facing Goliath will not soon forget that story from the Old Testament or the qualities that helped make a king. A lesson block may turn into a play performed by the children that might be shared with everyone in a school assembly. As a festival approaches, all the classes may start the day together, perhaps learning a song or hearing a story; afterward they might work on different parts of a pageant which are combined improvisationally for a festive occasion.

At Michaelmas, the whole children's Village may gather together for a harvest meal – no mean feat for a company of 150! All classes are busy with preparations. Everyone has something to contribute. Some classes bake bread; others harvest grapes and make juice. Perhaps one class will prepare a play for entertainment; another may practice songs. Many hands are needed to help make decora-tions. The older children help set up the room and lay the tables. The seniors serve the meal. Every-one brings something from autumn's bounty for the harvest altar.

The school life is rooted in an environment designed to support and enhance development of the children and to help them attain their individual potential. The extended family setting creates a supportive atmosphere, which instills a sense of security, offers individual guidance, and fosters social interrelationships. Physicians, nurses, and therapists recommend and carry out specific thera-pies directed toward the particular disabilities of the individual child.

Triform is the first Camphill training center in North America, located in a gentle rural landscape in the lower Hudson Valley. It is still in the early stages of its development and is presently a community of 35 people. It is a place where adolescents and young adults from 16–25 years of age with prob-lems of social maladjustment, emotional difficulties, and other special needs are offered a two-year program which provides them with work experience and work skills, social development, and further education.

Work training and experience is acquired at the organic farm and garden, where the fruits of the labor literally end up on the dinner table. In the household, cooking and housekeeping skills are learned. There is a carpentry workshop where training in woodworking also yields products that are sold for the community's livelihood.

The program of further education consists of academic courses and artistic activities. Eurythmy, drama, painting, and music encourage new modes of self-expression. Academic courses help to round-off incomplete educational backgrounds and open new areas of interest and understanding, as well as broaden world outlook.

In the evening the young people may participate in such activities as folk and choral singing, swimming, shopping, and discussion groups. There is a biweekly Triform meeting, a community forum, where major issues are discussed and decisions made.

There are three Camphill Villages for mentally handicapped adults in North America. You have already been guided around the largest and oldest of these, Camphill Village, Copake. Although it might well be representative of Village life, each center has its own distinct character.

Kimberton Hills is a sprawling, bustling community of approximately 115 people on a beautiful 430-acre farm in Pennsylvania. It is primarily an agricultural community operating a large bio-dynamic farm, which consists of field crops, vegetable and herb gardens, an orchard, a vineyard, soft-fruit plantings, cattle, poultry, sheep, and pigs. There is also a greenhouse, a dairy, a cheese house, as well as a bakery, which produces a variety of bread, some made from home-milled Village grain.

A farm store and a coffee shop are open for the public. Courses are offered in Social Therapy and agricultural training. The annual Kimberton Hills Agricultural Calendar is produced here. Village life in Kimberton is attuned to the cycle of the year and influenced by the rhythms of the farm.

Kimberton Hills has an active cultural life with several artists in residence. Here a wedding meal on the Village green is an especially festive occassion. It may include a scene from a play enacted by the bridegroom and bride. The Village choir will gather and perhaps a poem will celebrate the couple. Rose Hall Community Center is often the site for cultural events for the wider public. There could be an evening of classical music, a eurythmy performance, or a lecture on "The Cow." The bakery, coffee shop, and farm store, in close proximity to the hall, provides this Village with a lively and inviting center for social exchange with the surrounding community.

Lastly, there is Camphill Village, Minnesota. This is the most recent venture in North America. It is a rural community of about 25 people, still in its beginnings. Presently, there are three houses, a barn, a dairy, a trailer, a large implement shed, and a woodwork shop. The Village enjoys wide local support and interest, and among the pioneers, an enormous capacity for creative improvisation. The implement shed becomes a theatre for dramatic productions. A trailer bears the important title "The Home Bakery." A living room becomes, on Sunday, a chapel.

There is a rich program of activities to warm cold winter nights: plays, literature readings, speech, poetry, clay modelling, painting, and a weekly Village meeting. In summer the needs of the land prevail.

Life in Camphill Village, Minnesota is full of the hard work, neighborly interdependence, and tenacity characteristic of the midwest. It has also the enthusiasm and fire of the original impulse of Camphill.

Camphill is a way of life. It is not a job. There are no shifts, no salaries, no relative values placed on people according to the nature of the work that they do. But it is certainly a life full of jobs to be done. There are meals to cook, floors to sweep, fields to mow, cows to milk. There are children in need of special care. Tasks are undertaken for the good of the whole, out of a sense of commitment and responsibility. To be able to do real, meaningful work gives purpose and dignity to life.

Community life is the work of Camphill. People with enormously varied capabilities, talents, and needs, live and work together day after day. Competition loses its relevance. Diversity, not uniformity, becomes the standard; the uniqueness of the individual is the reality.

The well-being of the community is directly related to each member's willingness to contribute the best he can for the good of the whole, and regardless of that contribution, receive from the whole that which he needs. Each individual works to meet the needs of others, while in return his own needs are met. Rudolf Steiner describes this as the Fundamental Social Law. This is community building.

Wanda Root
Camphill Village, Copake

1   *Summer festival, Camphill Village, Copake, NY*

2 *Farm Complex, Copake*

3 *Columbine Pond, Copake* ▷

8   Karl König School House, Beaver Run ▷

7   Rainbow Hall Community Center, Beaver Run

9 ▷

△ 10 Rose Hall, Community Center, Kimberton Hills, PA

△ 11 Fountain Hall, Community Center, Copake, NY   12

13 "Oakhill" residence, Beaver Run

14   *School bell, Beaver Run*

15   *Beaver Run*

16

17

18

20

21

22   *Upper School, Beaver Run*

27 + 28 School Performance

29   *Curative Eurythmy Therapy, Beaver Run*

30

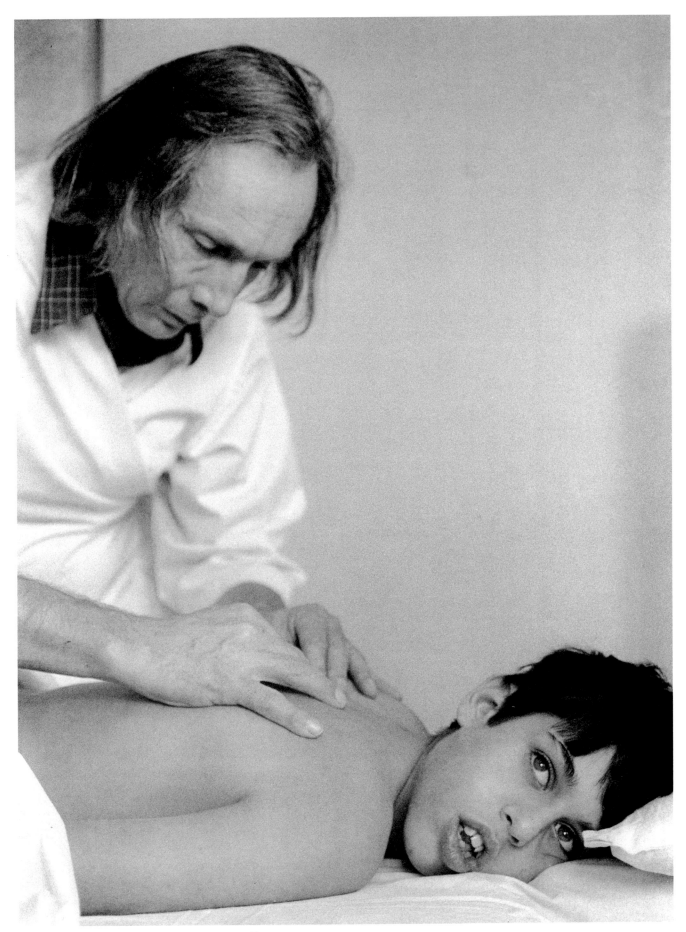

31   *Rhythmical Massage Therapy, Beaver Run*

32   Educational Eurythmy, Beaver Run

33 + 34   *School Assembly, Beaver Run*

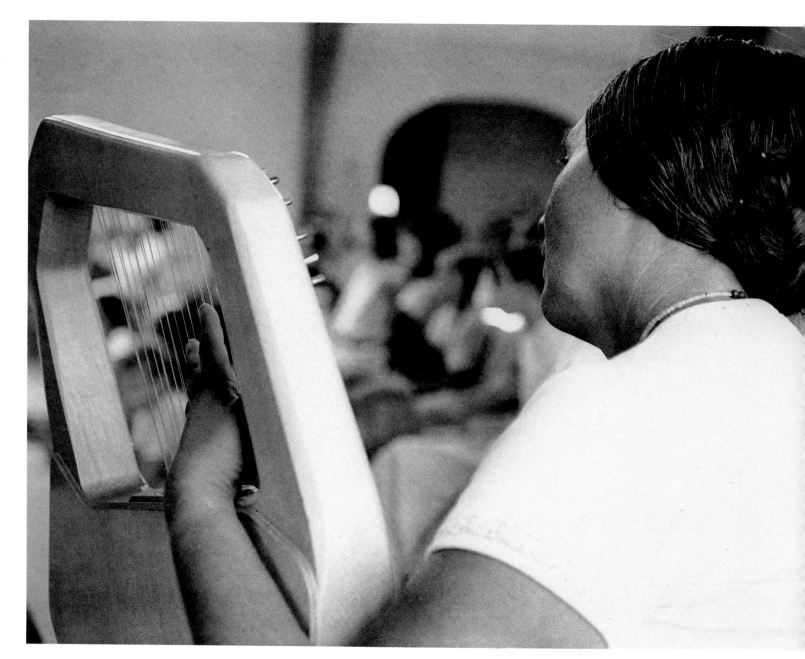

36   Riding Therapy, Beaver Run

38   *Making tomato sauce, Beaver Run*

39 + 40 Garden work, Ninth Grade, Beaver Run

48

41

49

42

43 + 44 Friendship, Beaver Run

45   *Cleanup around the Schoolhouse, Beaver Run*

46

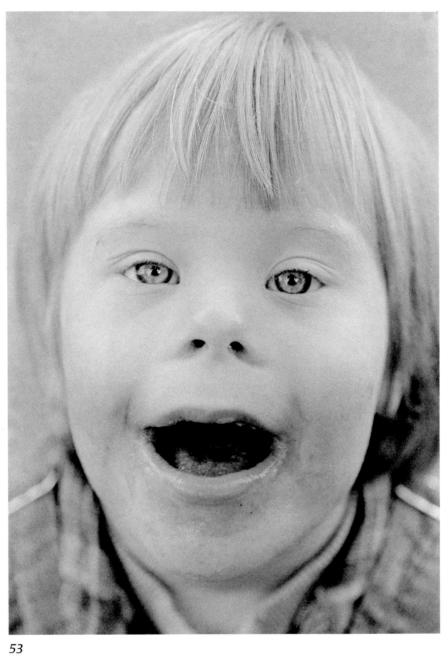

53

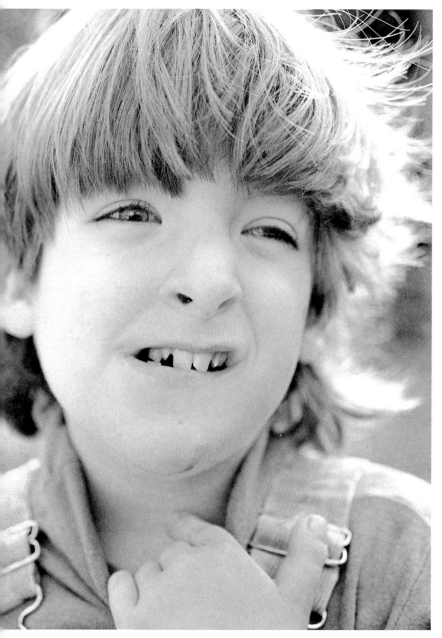

54 + 55

56

57

60

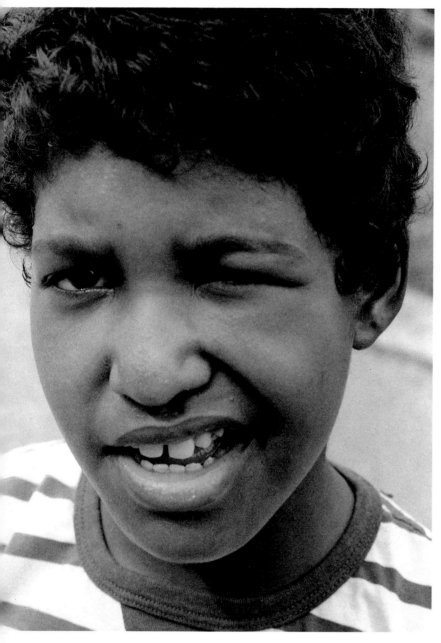

61 + 62

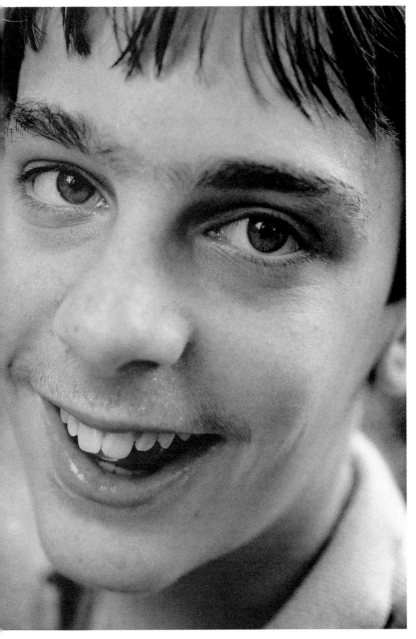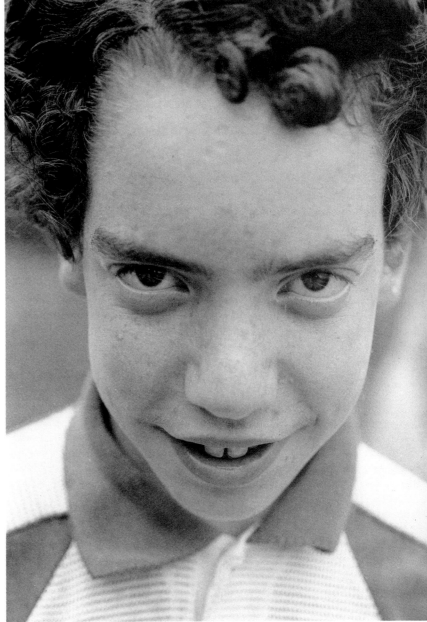

63 + 64

65

66

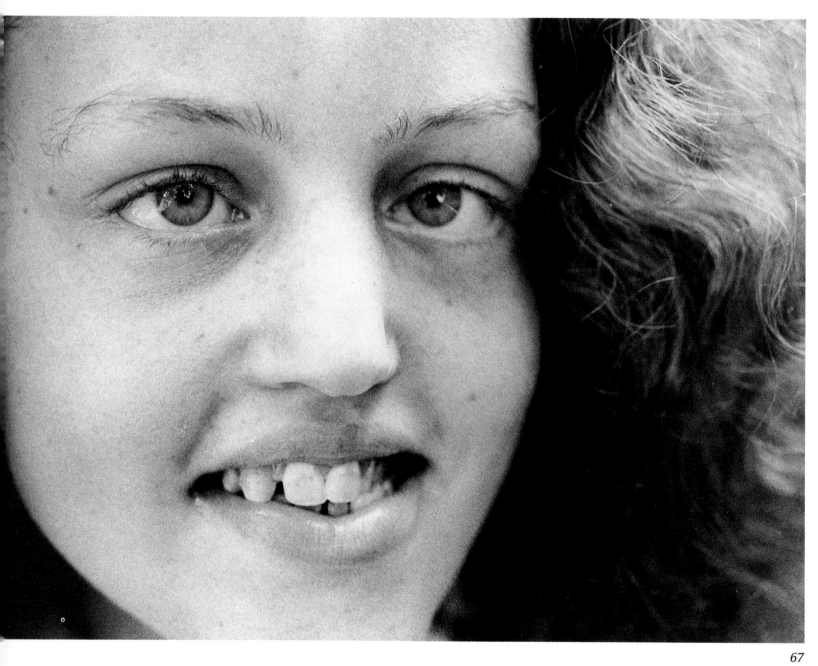

68

70

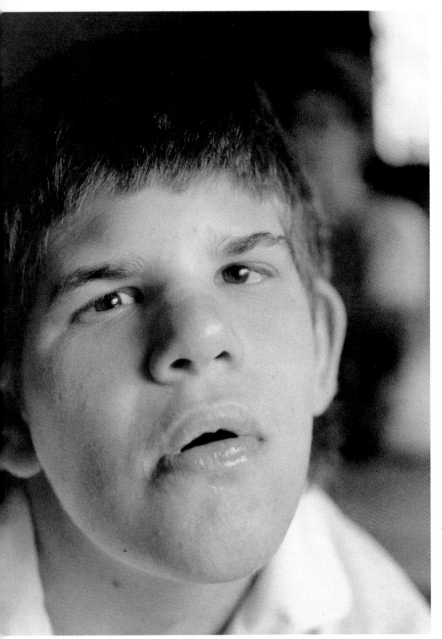 

71 + 72

73

77

79

80

82

83

85 + 86

87 + 88

89

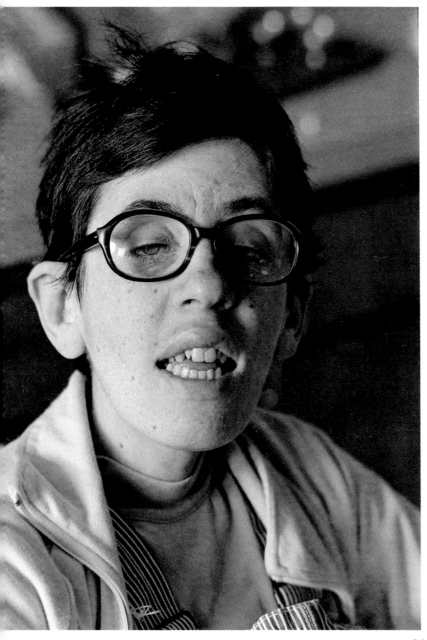 

90 + 91

92

94

98

99

101

103

105

106

107

109

110

111

112   Calendula garden, Kimberton Hills

113

115

116

117

118

119

122 + 123

124

125

126   Delivering garden produce, Copake

127 + 128

122

129   The onion harvest, Camphill Village, Minnesota

131

133

134

135   *Camphill Minnesota*

129

136   *Hay baling, Copake*

137

140

133

141

142

143

144   *Tapping the maple trees, Copake*

137

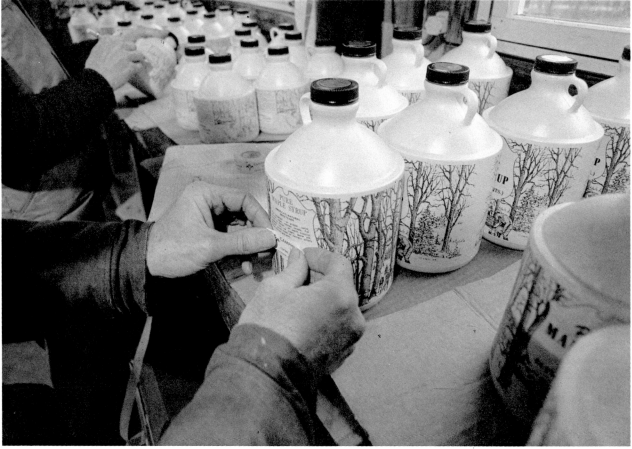

145 + 146   *Processing maple syrup, Copake*

147

148   *Woodshop, Triform, Hudson, NY*

149

151 *Enamel craftshop, Copake*

143

152 *Beeswax candles, Copake*

153   *Batik craftshop, Copake*

155   The weavery, Copake

156

157

149

159 + 160   Summer harvest, vegetable/herb garden

151

161   *Tomato distribution for the houses, Copake*

163 + 164   The apple orchard, Kimberton Hills

154

165

166 Onion delivery, Copake

167

168   Night fishing, Minnesota

169

170   The summer season, Kimberton Hills

171

173   *Village meeting, Minnesota*

174

175

176   Second year seminar celebration, Beaver Run

177

178   *St. John's summer festival, Copake*

183

184

185

174

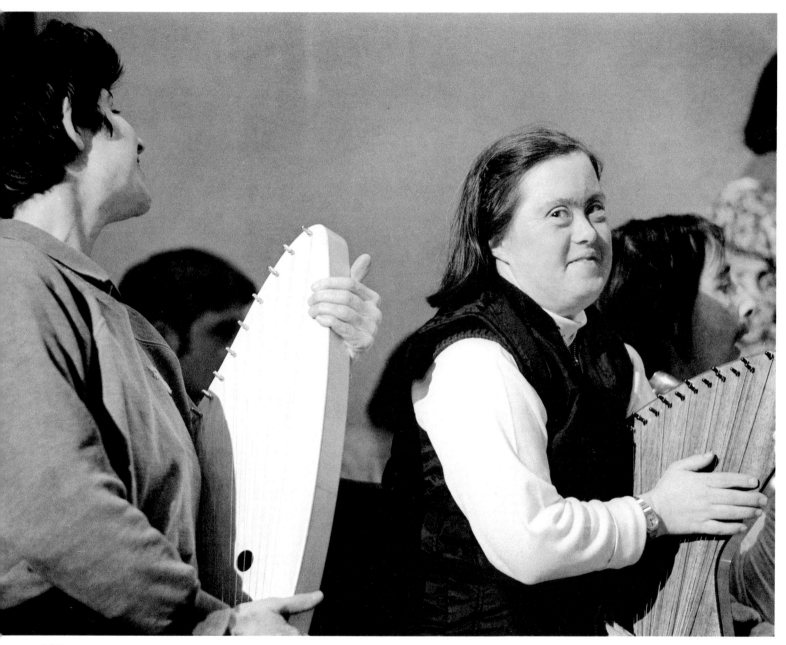

186

187   *Choir, Fountain Hall, Copake*

188

189

177

190 + 191 Michaelmas celebration, Beaver Run

192 + 193 Copake

179

194 + 195

196   *Michaelmas meal, Copake*

197 + 198   Shrove Tuesday/Mardi Gras, Beaver Run

182

199 + 200

201 Dance around the Maypole, Beaver Run

WHO ARE THESE PEOPLE?

*They are the hostages we surrendered long
        ago to ransom a future;
They are a clear reflection and a continuous
        confirmation of the very best part of ourselves;
They are that divine dividend, the long promised
        blessing reserved for those among us who have
        never seen but have always believed;
They are a promise kept, a hope fulfilled,
        a dream realized;
They are a manifestation of the profound love that
        governs the universe, a love perpetually nourished
        by the realization of itself, and a love surrendered
        over and over again in joy and gratitude at the
        command of the omnipotent spirit.
They are you and me!*

Martin Sheen

VILLAGE LIFE *Carlo Pietzner*

There had been a symposium in town with the topic "The handicapped and their habitation." It had been the last of a series of seminars, the last before the college would finally succumb to the stupor of heat and its annual lassitude. It was an intelligent company which tried to reach beyond simplistic concepts of integration, segregation and normalization to their vital challenge in the greater social and moral context. Of necessity the symposium had to deal with the notion of deviation, with the developmentally disabled perceived as deviants from some acceptable norms.

One aspect of the discussion turned from the question of using existing housing for single, retarded people to using so-called group homes. This latter position was the most fervently represented, the more fervent where the memory of the huge asylum-type of institution lingered.

There were other voices, however, which argued for dwellings which would be especially developed to compensate for specific inner and outer deficiencies in the handicapped individual. These would be homes and groups of houses with a greater regard for their occupants. It was interesting to hear the first of these arguments — about houses adapted for apartments and group homes — much more forcefully delivered, though very often with scant experience of real situations. The other, much more fragmented, group had a harder time making itself understood, almost as if its members themselves belonged to a somewhat impaired group. Altogether the enormous fund of creative, even healing, activity offered through work on the land, whether as farm work or through work in gardens and greenhouses, was almost completely left unexplored. This kind of healing activity even seemed somehow degrading when considered through the lens of professional scrutiny.

Having these different thoughts in mind, it was pleasant to return to the village. It was still. Hot summer flickered around the shadows where the trees march up the hills. Only a few birds could be heard, for after St. John's Day most of the singing ceases. Yet from the distance a voice could be heard. This was unusual, for at noon everyone was at home eating lunch. The singing voice, however, was nearing steadily, but came without hurry and with no fear of reproach. The singer was a woman. She soon became visible entering the shady lane which runs at the foot of the hill past the little hall-pond. She had spread out her arms as if accepting the summer into herself and now one could recognize that she sang at the top of her jubilant voice: "Ho-oly night, silent night!"

Somehow, the idea of Christmas had occured to her as part of her inner, more flexible and more important habitation. The summer light seemed to carry her and make her swim toward her house at the end of the lane. She was about as integrated as one would imagine a person can be. True, she would have been bewildering anywhere else, but not here. She presented some questions, certainly. She would have cut a somewhat strange figure, liable to be exploited in the subway or in the supermarket. Her singing, accompanied by sprays of spittle, may have caused resentment. But the most important question seemed to be: what was it that made this summer-Christmas-song so human? Contrary to the symposium, the topic in our village seemed to be: can we teach humaness? If so, all our handicaps could find a suitable habitation.

In the evening the cooler air brought about a lively conversation among several people who had heard the arguments offered at the symposium. The scrutiny continued about the concept, realization, and development of that entity called *village*. The questioning turned to the heart of the matter itself: what *is* a village? Can it be made to grow organically as if from seeds? Is it a deliberately planned artifact from its very beginning? How is the village different say, in Middle-Europe, Greece, or in Africa (whose settlements always remained rather small)? What role, if any, did the village as a social element play in America (where everything has the tendency to grow large)? An early argument was made against the effective influence of such a small transplanted assemblage as a village by recalling a question Saul Bellow brought forward in his story *A Silver Dish*: "How was it that the accumulated gripes of all the ages took off so when transplanted to America?" *1)

For transplanted the village was, at least in the differentiated forms which were common in Europe. The slow growth of this social entity had given validity and texture to the fabric of communal life in Middle-Europe. This cannot be said of the United States, at least not as a widespread pattern for the nation. *2)

At this point the conversation turned toward the modern relevance of these questions. The way in which the settlement density of our village had come about seemed to puzzle some participants. Was it because the village, eager to grow, looked around for "recruits?" Or was it because strangers felt a new security at the place to which they had chanced to come? Did the village call on newcomers? Did the newcomers determine the manner of growth of the place? And what relevance did all this have to America, not only for the way historically in which America became a land of settlers, but for today, perhaps even for the future when different social values from the present might supercede those we are accustomed to now?

Did *we* really know what a village was? What need and longing did it satisfy? It seemed a little clearer how villages came about, at least in Middle-Europe. But when did they reach village status? And when did they pass from a village to a town? When does a town become a city? Is it really only a matter of size? Was the very village in which these conversations took place, and whose life concerned the speakers every day and hour, a given, an outwardly determined structure? Or was it a deliberate creation, no longer with the sap of the 'familia' as its incentive, but a creation of a new 'familia?' Was this not a gathering of diverse people sharing not only existential needs, but the resolute attempt to participate in the vicissitudes and compassions of an inner life with people in need of special care and understanding?

It was here that the puzzlement had its true location. For it seemed to have to deal with a monstrous contradiction: on the one hand, the impulse to seek out and build up a habitation which could satisfy the need for a truly communal life; and on the other hand, the isolating influence focussed in the irrepressible demand for individualism. *3)

The night was still transparent but, it now seemed, without sound. Then the crickets lowered their sawing like a curtain of noise, behind which the frogs, to which no attention had been given until then, began *their* glorious symposium. The conversants departed with the promise to continue at a later date.

When this happened a few days later, more people heard of the gathering and joined the company. Early on someone quoted from Bader's book about villages *4). There were village-designations of great variety from *familia abbatis* to *corporation,* to *universitas* or to *communitas.* The most fitting for present-day seemed to be: *village community.*

The question concerning identity arose again with these descriptions. What size and structure would make a village slide over into a different form? This form would be larger and already by the usage of the name "town" suggest a different origin altogether. Somebody promised to consult Webster on this. *5)

It was more than an academic interest for us to seek our way through that grey zone of nouns, all of which seemed flexible, and, ultimately, unspecific. There are many such nouns, but some cannot be dispensed with, such as hamlet, village, town, city and possibly municipality. As citizens of our time we think of truly modern conglomerations in terms of city, capital and metropolis. The vision of the future for America is the megalopolis, stretching along the seaboard from Boston to Washington, D.C. or from San Francisco to Los Angeles.

The mere accumulation of people and their houses, farms and barns, stables and shops — in other words just growth — seemed altogether too mechanistic a principle for determining a hamlet, village, town city or metropolis. Swelling beyond a boundary, from an original focus into some less ordered outreach, seemed more like a barely governable epidemic than a deliberate construct.

Do people form buildings or do buildings form people? It is startling to hear that the borders of lordly estates, forests, fields, banks of streams (also state and national borders) did not determine the settlement of villages in the Middle Ages. Villages determined the borders and the border country.

A call sent out to assemble in order to perform a summer-pageant interrupted the conversation at this point. Everyone was to participate in the pageant. Even guests and visitors would be invited to play their part, parts without words perhaps, or at most an attempt to join a speech-chorus or a song. The pageant consisted of four sections, each of which was to be played at a different location. When it was performed for the first time the community hall was not yet built. There was only a huge, crater filled with slate, and in the shattered pieces of rock, pyrites or fool's gold glittered in the sun. Many of those present experienced the building that was planned for this site as if its walls, roof, and windows were already visible.

Soon the community and its visitors found their places, some in elaborate costumes, others in their everyday outfits. Players began to cluster at the four principal points of the pageant. Everyone not wearing a costume was garlanded by a circlet of flowers, at times by a white, yellow and green wreath, or with a posy knotted to freshly-cut canes. A reticent onlooker might simply carry a branch, broken from the ample hedgerows and underbrush.

The first stop was at the bottom of the farm hill. The two figures of Abraham and Melchizedek met surrounded by their retinue. Each humble follower of the King of Jerusalem brought a small loaf of bread. They were received with reverence by Abraham, his household and servants. Except for the costumed participants who had remained at their prescribed places, everybody had assembled and now moved on together to the second act.

The participants stopped inside a ring of stately trees, where a small, square monument stands, made of Alabama limestone and topped by a gilded pyramidal roof. They filled the enclosure and watched children dressed in colorful garments representing the elements of earth, water, air and fire. Pan appeared with his simple flute, to die amidst the elements. The whole of nature was to respond to his death and Echo, the nymph, was to witness the faltering and dwindling of his music. Music itself was to continue for further aspirations of the human soul. For the third act, everyone walked to the pond, near the site where the community hall would stand. Monks and knights appeared, and while they do not belong to the origins of this country, they do belong to the unconscious pulse of a history we all share. To become more human is not bound to the traditions of nations, or their folk-tales, sagas and legends. For they belong to all of us and people should not be cut off from them because they are chiefly found across the oceans or the mountains.

The Being of Music was rowed in a boat across the pond to the opposite shore — her new habitat. Everyone assembled there once more, standing on the enormous rim of the building site. Right in the center of the crater-like dish, frail and vulnerable, stood a small harpsichord, upon which a musician with the likeness of Mozart played and at which he received the Being of Music. The culmination occurred when the musician led everyone in the chorus of: "In these most sacred walls, revenge is quite unknown..."

This occurred before the hall was built, and the words and songs confirmed that the hall would be rendered in such a way as to express by its very form, structure, and usefulness the core intentions of this village. A central building is the crystal and epitome of all the other edifices of a village. It is a center which embodies and declares the purposes of such a deliberate foundation as a modern village. Provisional space in our village served as the community gathering place for almost 10 years — until everyone was ready for the hall. It became the focal and gathering point for the village with natural ease.

One imagines the central point of a circle to be the most exclusive, while in reality it contains the whole circumference. This becomes even more obvious with the experience of such an edifice as the village hall. Everyone who comes to visit the village can see it. Anybody who sees the hall can experience the whole village. The building, huge, yet filled with clear purpose in every nook and cranny, is at once wide open and gently sheltering. It's Indian-red surface flames brightly through the foliage, majestically so in autumn. Its forms, though unusual, have behind them the tradition of organic liveliness which comes from a whole school of architecture in reinforced concrete. This is practiced from Middle-Europe and Scandinavia to Japan, and its first practitioner was Rudolf Steiner. This building would not want to compete with other models of buildings borrowed from the past. What about *new* structures for work and worship based on a *new* conception of social integration, of living and working together?

Many people are familiar with this village hall by now. This afternoon it had once again received almost the whole assembly of villagers from the oldest to the youngest, as well as many visitors — a good deal more than 200 people.

In the evening the participants in the village conversation gathered again on the large porch of one of the houses. The afternoon's event in the hall was found to have had a profoundly sacramental character without in the slightest degree calling up what is usually understood as a religious practice. The drawing power of the hall had played its solemn and its joyful part and had given the impression that one was in the presence of an ordering principle and a balancing agent. If this was an enthusing thought it was also a sobering one. Questions arose again concerning the relevance of history regarding the modern vision of the village. Just as other elements which went into the establishment of villages were of the past the aspect of the central building also contained both historical precedence and present-day challenges. As Bader describes it: "...for the village congregation in the Middle Ages, as for the village itself, the church constituted the natural center. The church court was village-forming, even in regions which offered impediments such as settlements in steep mountain regions. For the peasant of the late Middle-Ages the church as a whole is the mediator of religious blessing and of a transition from a toilsome earthly life to an eternal one. The village church is also the scene and theater of festive, celebrating acts. The villager's processions lead from the church into the fields and plains. The church courtyard is also, in a very real sense, an asylum, where one seeks protection against lordly strife within its walls and lastly in the donjon. The yard is a place of judgement and assembly under the village linden-tree, particularly if neither a tavern nor a gaming-place is available to the congregation. In the churchyard one also builds cellars and store-rooms in order to have provisions in wartime and also in hope of finding protection against thieves and robber-gangs in that hallowed area. Far more importantly, the churchyard is first of all a place for burial. Still moved by tribal and 'familia' thinking, one is together there with one's 'own' dead, whose bones lie piled up after the allotted time for 'the peace of the grave' has passed. A last reference for one's ancestors lives in this communion of the living and the dead." *6)

There was some clatter at the back of the house. The screen door opened and fell shut again with bang. The persons who appeared through it had their hands full. A young lady, with stubby fingers daintily spread under a tray with glasses, spoke with the voice of an ideal Edwardian butler antici-pating refreshments for her lordships. She had a deep voice and her fair hair stood as if it were a wreath left from the pageant. Her grin was so luminous that it could almost be seen in the dark, like the rise of the moon before its appearance over the horizon. The other person, a very tall man in pajamas, was perhaps 35 years of age. He had rolled his trousers up to his knees. True, the day had been extremely hot, but the night air was cool. He handed his tray over as soon as he could find a pair of willing hands. It was filled with fragrant bread which the village bakery produced, and accom-panied by a slab of butter. He stood like a statue, smiled, and said: "Go on!"

"Yes, please," said the young woman with a still deeper voice. She handed the glasses carefully to each member of the assembly. "Would it not be time to sleep?" someone asked her. "No, no," she said emphatically, "I want to hear about our church, too." The tall gentleman, standing motionless, fell in with her. "Yes," he added. "The hall."

We continued with Bader's discussion of the desire of the village to have a church of its own.

"A village without a church is not a real, fully acceptable village. It is quite possible to fulfill the demand to be present every Sunday at mass, but this can also be done in the neighboring village. Yet a chapel was not really enough; that is, just a sacramental house with a consecrated altar. What was wanted was a complete and full church and the villagers were prepared to pay for it, too. But in the absence of such a church, the villagers were attached far more closely to their own chapel, than to an admirable edifice next door, so to speak. If the absence of such a building persisted, parti-cularly in smaller villages, it became their first and major interest as the population increased. It was often a matter of real sacrifice to go ahead with the building against all odds; the fitting out, conse-cration and care of a village-chapel. The latter involved the appointment of a suitable person and where such could not be found, they weighed up the overlap of certain duties. The care of the church or chapel could be entrusted to, say the village-builder, the village judge and others." *7)

We were reminded of the close relationship people had to their skills or trade in the Middle Ages. It impregnated them. It became so fused with their persona that people even took their names from it. The village smith later became Mr. Smith; Mr. Baker was the baker; Mr. Miller the much needed specialist handling the grain's reduction to flour and so forth. Crafts were givers of names; they described life in the village as it was then. People became one – possessed almost – with their work. When the settlement grew so large that there were more than one miller, baker or smith, a regular market would often take place in the village square and with it the designation 'town' began to intrude on the village.

191

"Let me digress for a moment," said another voice. In response the young woman sat down loudly on the porch and folded her legs with ease in a position others try for a long time to acquire without too much pain and distraction. "It's to do with the church," she said in her deep voice. The tall man continued to stand statue-like in the midst of the group and reinforced her remark by saying, "Its the hall, yes, the hall. Go on!"

"In December, 1980 the Polish philosopher and writer Leszek Kolakowski received the 'Prize of the European Essay' of the Charles-Veillon-foundation of Lausanne. The lecture which Kolakowski gave at this occasion was called: The Undiscoverable Village. *8) It was a remarkable lecture and it had a remarkable beginning. Roughly translated, Kolakowski started off by saying:

"From time to time we hear that we have found ourselves in a gigantic village which stretches over the whole surface of the earth. Thanks to an unbelieveable expansion of the information media it is felt as if we would have restored the village — after the destruction of the traditional village — through a "dialectic" spiral but now of global size and measure. However, this opinion is hardly credible; in fact, the opposite judgement seems to be better founded: there is no 'spiral,' there is only an irresistable movement in one direction, which year after year erases the traces of the rural communities and whose successes are highly visible in the town (or city) culture of the industrialized world. This village monster, whose inhabitants we occasionally imagine ourselves to be, is the opposite of the old village, and not only in its technology. The peasant economy had once been a perfect model of recycling, so that the agricultural economy hardly had to deal with garbage. Everything was used again, while with our civilization this problem has reached embarrassing proportions. But we are not dealing here with the giddy rhythms of change which so clearly contrasts with the monotonous cycle of rural life. We deal rather with a purely imagined, totally artificial village, a cerebral substitute which can only with difficulty be concealed in its unreality, and which, under a number of ideological guises, increasingly creates a nostalgia for the 'real village'!"

The stillness which followed was tense. The young lady was a little bored. She had found a piece of string which she twiddled ingeniously between three of her fingers. She seemed far away, but not for lack of an adequate attention span, rather because the subject she had come for had been further obscured as far as she was concerned.

"Just one further quote from Kolakowsky," the eager voice continued. Here it is:

"We are torn between two irreconcilable desires: we want the state less and less, whose supervision of, and obtrusive interference in, our affairs angers us, and who lets us feel our weakness only too clearly. At the same time we want ever more from the state, which should also protect us against any mishaps, whether they may derive from nature, from society, or ourselves. The state shall give us complete security by bothering about our interests and shall defend our particular interest against all other interests.

This schizophrenic stance is best expressed in the ultra left ideologies which promise us that when their representatives have attained power everything in society will be satisfactorily planned and at the same time everything will be spontaneous."

In response to this quotation someone said:

"This already belongs to the governance of the village. Are we ready for this? Should we not deal, as we set out to do, with the building up of a village, its modern relevance and the awareness of such aspects which seem to have — if not an eternal — then at least a timeless character?"

"The concept of a global village makes me shudder," said a gentle, female voice. "When I lived in New York you could experience ethnic villages clustered together in a huge conglomeration. From the big avenues you stepped into an enclave of wholly German customs and nostalgias. If by chance you ventured to the right, you were engulfed by the Irish, and green-painted shamrocks were everywhere. To the left were Scandinavians and Moroccans, and so on. The zone of transition between different groups was almost nonexistent. Everything was close together, but without forming an organic entity. An inadvertent step made you surface in a village of another continent. By this, the global concept assumes a similar character, only more homogeneous by default and convenience. The diversities of the past would gradually become a monstrous village accessory of the global village whose task would merely be to grow into one enormous body. I cannot help it but I see it like an alligator, or better still, a dragon. The global village can be achieved, even made inevitable, with the aid of complete saturation by the media. Anything *they* regard as worthy or opportune to communicate would forget links for this global village. I suppose the owners of the principal TV stations could manipulate this and their listeners at will. The momentum of this creepy beast and its consuming power is enormous. It makes itself appear reasonable with progress on its side. We must be aware that efforts not conforming to the trend of homogeneity will be regarded as odd, suspicious, contrary, segregating or even hostile."

It had now become late, although further conversations were still clearly needed. The young lady and the statuesque man behind her nodded agreement and began to leave. The man, however, rolled his pajama legs down rather brusquely, as if to show that his expectation of wading through some kind of tangible enlightenment had been disappointed.

*

The next weeks in the village were unexpectedly diverting through duties and difficulties arising from complex word-keeping and classification requirements. Only very few of the most enlightened regulatory agencies had been able to free themselves and our village from the plethora of suffocating paperwork despite their professed preference for seeing those with developmental disabilities join the ranks of the "normal."

Colder nights prevented the group from gathering in the open. The first fall colors began to consume the still dark-green trees at the most vulnerable places of their circumference. September sounded its earnest call for the return from vacation-vacancy. Michaelmas was on its way with conscious resolutions and earnest endeavors.

In addition to other Michaelmas celebrations, there was to be a harvest meal at noon prepared by the farmers and gardeners. Oblong hay-bales were neatly piled together in a wide semicircle before the entrance to the barn loft.

Below, in the partially unroofed pen, one could hear the pigs jostling each other. Some of the cows grazed with four horses in the fields behind, and pigeons flew in and out of the barn, no longer followed by darting swallows. Villagers and co-workers began to assemble. Here and there were natural families, some with infants, and at other places the larger, deliberately composed families, all a far cry from the 'familia' of the past. They sat down on the bales. Bread, cheese, fruit and pitchers of fruit juice were carried around by eager helpers. Speeches were given, some matching in exuberance the practised eloquence of others. A choir sang. Gratitude flowed amongst the participants as if it were a visible stream of air, touching everyone.

A latecomer could have made a startling observation. The hay-bales had been set in a strict semicircular way which gave to the large area and its inviting loft space the feeling of an additional building set into the farmstead's welcoming wings. That there were people sitting on each of these oblong bolsters made the impression of walls made of hay and people even more vivid. Only a roof was missing to complete this picture.

Some kind of order of a planetary nature was at work in an almost playful way. Everything seemed to move around points of sustaining power and it became clear that even here the central building of the hall had found an expressive echo in the walls of people, in a linkage of living building blocks. The latecomer would notice that he or she had been missing in that stirring structure, just as even now one area of bales not yet claimed by anyone, left a noticeable gap in the form. Form, at the holiest times a vessel, and at other moments a persuader, is like the trace of invisible beings who walk amongst us to leave some imprint of their higher order upon those forms which we offer. Forms once spoke. Their language sounded through the church and its yard in the villages of the Middle Ages. Forms helped their inhabitants to speak to each other and were reminders of an exactitude beyond mere reason.

When the festivity was over the whole magical image of a living building fell immediately into disarray. Some people started to jostle one another as if no longer wisely guided by the multihanded influence of form. Others tried to intervene. There was impatience and disagreement. It was not a festival of peace at this juncture any longer. The task of pacification and reconciliation had to begin again. Those who left silently had been equally affected by the loud, if limited, tumult. A village is no substitute for paradise. It is, rather, a kind of guide through life, when ways have been lost...*9)

The thinker of these thoughts saw himself suddenly walking alone on the ringroad like some of the villagers who had been disturbed by the quarrel. He reached one of the slower-walking villagers, a very short, young woman with pronounced teeth, who walked with her head bent, wearing a cap of dangling flaps which looked like blinkers. She was not looking at the flecks of color with which the late sun had begun to glow over the hills. "Sad?" he asked. The face lifted itself; her eyes were still clouded behind the circumscribed land of words at her disposal. "We didn't sing," she whispered, "n-no--no popper grace." She was right. The abruptness of the end of Michaelmas meal had contributed to the quick and careless abandonment of the hay-bale-house. He firmly agreed with her. "Will you come to supper?" he asked. Now the light reached almost into her eyes, or was it the smile? "Can't," she responded. "Must make a n-ni-nice dinner table for St. Michael." It was clear that no further argument was possible. Certainly, Michaelmas had come.

That same evening there was a festive gathering in the hall. It seemed natural that the conversation afterwards turned once more to questions of modern villages. There were two or three people there who had been present at the very beginnings of our community. It was of interest to hear what the *original impulse* had been and how they had begun to root themselves in an evolutionary matrix. Questions were freely asked.

"What was first: the decision to form a community or to build a village?"

"Forming a community went together with the conviction that we could and would only pursue it with a specific task, a social service of some kind, which would occupy us at least as much as matters of the community. As yet there was no thought of a village, particularly as our concerns were with children, often rather severely handicapped ones. Later, when these children became older, "a suitable environment seemed to be vested in village forms. It was the children – no longer children – who called forth the actual development of villages."

"Many villages have been developed following the original impulse of providing help and work based on a spiritual image of the human being, however tortured. Some of these villages, often because they were developed in rural settings, derived their activities through work on the land. For almost all of them it would be correct to say that the children came first. These children called for teachers and farmers whose *own* lives now began to turn to those of the whole community. A need for therapeutic support was soon added. Here lies the moment in time when a village with handicapped children sprang into life. From its inception this children's village tried to be more than a strictly educational environment and it succeeded in part. It was through the variety and balance of disciplines and leisure in this situation which helped to mould it into a village."

"It must have been a very special idea to develop a children's village. It was a new kind of undertaking and almost contrary to previous experiences in the field."

"That this should have happened is one of the most exciting results of slowly accumulating convictions and insights. The *attitude* in a children's village must be a completely different one from a village for adults. The former kind of village – for children – is steeped in, and determined by, education. In the past this was developed after a central building, then mostly the chapel or church, had come into existence. To equip houses and grounds and other necessities for work and life in a residential setting with children leads very rapidly into a dichotomy between teachers and their own life-styles (including their families) and those who are taught, however brilliantly and humanely the teachers and houseparents act. Education as such remains a specific area with specific tasks and does not give rise to a full and undivided life as is natural for a village. The idea of the children's village tried to remedy this. The emphasis would be on education, but at least the village invited all those living there to join in a common venture of sharing. The village concept can be discerned from the educational side. In the future the 'total' or 'complete' village will always need a school and other educational elements built into it. With village-building everything has to be learned. Shall there be *one* complete village or perhaps several contiguous ones or separate villages each with different, specific tasks?"

Two participants of the conversation detached themselves from the group and continued the discussion while walking on the ringroad around the village. One of them took the topic further.

"The conscious decision to live differently and not be drawn into the compulsions of the larger population stands at the founding of every modern village. This decision is a tribute to the different needs of mankind, some of which must be taken *into* the very core of village existence. The onus of integration lies on the village and not only on the individual."

"But is not educational work with children so one sided as to exclude the village idea?"

"You must appreciate that it was around children that the village idea first had a comeback in our time. Born out of appalling needs, hunger, illness, desertion and the whole gruesome itinerary of cruelty and pain, it became apparent that the sheer numbers of children within a comparably small circumference called for sustained and adequate means of support. It was far more important to *do* something and to do it at once, however deficient it might be. This is still the same today." *10)

The two speakers found themselves walking the ringroad for the third time. Along its side a number of well-proportioned houses seemed to converse with the leaves that by now gave out a dry autumnal music as the wind played through them.

"How is it with the festivals?" asked the younger of the men. "We have gradually learned how important they are and how much depends on the initiative and participation by the villagers so that each festival comes alive. Teachers and houseparents may do a lot to make a festive mood permeate a school assembly or a Saturday evening, but the children themselves? Does not the most important and modern aspect of a village — that of active participation in the festivals — lie in this sphere?"

"Have you ever gone to a place where the presence of children is dominant when it was Advent, or better still at Christmas? This is *their* time. Pentecost; high summer with St. John's Day at the beginning, and when his decapitation is recalled at the end; Michaelmas; these belong to the kind of village with adults in mind. Where there is a preponderance of children, stars become visible again as patterns of light and influence. Stillness can become a living friend; songs and the telling of stories spread around like a climate."

*

At Christmas in the children's village there seemed to be a mood of hushed concentration. The village was putting on the Oberufer Nativity Play. There was a "star singer" who welcomed the audience. There was an angel, Mary, and Joseph who leaned on his stick, old, but steadfast. Most important for building bridges between this holy grouping and the audience — with children sitting in front — were the sheperds, almost like guardians of the village-idea.

One must still speak of a culminating subject if we consider village life. It is about a figure who is now rarely seen and could soon disappear into the peculiar shrouds which, one after the other, veil people and events until they are wrapped in what we call history. This figure has a remarkable strength with which to pluck our heartstrings. We feel him to be pervasive even in his absence. In the past he was to be found in every village; there were sometimes more than one together. He is the shepherd. *[11])

Is there a shepherd in the modern village? For if not, let history be history. Obviously there *are* shepherds in certain villages of certain countries, but they carry out a traditional and limited sequence of duties.

"The shepherds of the Nativity Play seem to be an archetype. Somehow their intonation of life embraces humanity's earthly sojourn in such ways as to make a wonder of childhood and of motherhood, of endurance in adversity, of middle and of old age — the whole majestic repertoire of mankind."

Sometime later the two men met again in conversation *[12]), the younger one accompanying a handsome slender girl with long hair closely brushed around her Indian face. She had come to work in the village only a short time ago and much that was said was new to her. A good deal was spoken about the Christmas festival at the children's village. Certainly, one could feel some of its after effects, even now, when the snow had begun to melt and the first signs of spring could be detected. The three walked along the low stone wall. Lilac colored raspberry spurs erupted along the way and small, round depressions in the snow made them look as if standing on individual dishes. Halfhearted handfulls of crumbling snow flaked from the pines.

The young man began to speak: "But what about..." and the older one finished for him: "Easter? You did mean Easter, did you not?" The young woman nodded emphatically as if she would have been addressed. "Yes, Easter!"

"When we know how, where and with whom to celebrate Easter, our village will be what it longs to be: a habitation for the whole human being. Michaelmas will have taken place, Advent and Christmas will have followed in the light of the child. But Easter is the festival of the individual, an appreciation through loneliness, a celebration of humility and compassion all of one's own. It can resolve the contradiction of individuality which needs at the same time a community form. Any true individual gain can only be accomplished if it is at the same time a furthering of the community."

*

One can conclude with a quotation – prophetic – but no less real because of it, and a summation of much that was said. It is from a lecture by Rudolf Steiner, at Dornach, Switzerland, August 7, 1920. "People have yet to realize the magnitude of the coming upheavals; this is only a lull between the last catastrophy and the next one. The souls sleeping during this respite will have a rude awakening one day. They will rub their eyes and pull off their sleeping caps when the catastrophy continues on its course. Yet, what will work its way to the surface despite all this is the village community. Only a person who understands the nature of the individual village communities comprehends what is trying to emerge in the East as a social constitution. The village community is the only reality in the East. All the rest is but an institution that is perishing.

It will be the task of people in the West to understand the means by which this aggregate of the village community can be organized. Indeed, the West's web of opinions, which is being trapped in the single human individualities, can also be organized only by the Threefold Social Organism. (Editor: See *The Threefold Social Order,* Rudolf Steiner 1919, Anthrophosophic Press 1966.) On the one hand, the Threefold Social Organism must incorporate the individual members of the eastern village communities. On the other hand it must save from ruin the crumbling western organisms that are becoming individualized and which, as aggregates, are splitting up into their seperate components."

Carlo Pietzner

FOOTNOTES AND COMMENTS:

1)   Saul Bellow. *Him with his foot in his mouth.* Pocket Books, New York, October 1985.

2)   For the description of the European relative of the village, indeptedness must be acknowledged for the volume which concerns itself with just these questions. *Village-Association and Village-Congregation* focusses its investigations chiefly on the Middle Ages. The book is in German: *Dorfgenossenschaft und Dorfgemeinde* by Karl Siegfried Bader, Boehlau Verlag, Köln, Graz, 1962. Some samples: "In fact, rights and privileges, but also duties and obligations of villages were formulated at the period of the Middle Ages, which at the same time constituted the archaic period of village development. These were determined by the 'house,' which also meant familia or family."
"It seems almost self-understood that with the decision to settle near others and to live together in peace or strife, the need arises for neighborly relationships and regulated associations. Without them, a healthy life together did not seem possible, and the means to achieve this became ever more elaborate."
"In this early epoch of organized life, a stranger who wanted to settle in the precincts of a village could no longer be kept away (as was done still earlier). One's neighbor, whether he belonged to one's own 'familia' or not, could no longer be treated as a stranger."
"These processes led beyond the old neighborly community forms toward the actual village form, though very gradually, for they depended on the processes of settlement-density."

3)   A telling reminder was offered at this juncture. Quoting Thornton Wilder: "[Emerson] was — to use a much admired phrase — sufficient to himself. And here we are back to our American individualism. That's what American individualism is: sufficiency to oneself. That Americans are also lonely and hence insufficient to themselves is only apparently a contradiction: for they are sufficient to themselves without being able to make that sufficiency into a sufficiency to the whole experience of life which includes themselves."
From the journals of Thornton Wilder, N.Y. Tuesday, November 6, 1985, Columbia University Club: Emerson's Optimism (and America's) from: the *New Criterion*, Vol. 4/No2/Oct. 1985.

4)   The gradual concentration of houses and settlements did not prove viable enough to grow into a full-fledged village everywhere. But where it led to strong densities a conflux and unity between a specific task, (say, the culture of vineyards) with the appropriate forms of labor can be discovered. Where a fully-fledged village form is reached, the people and families belonging to that settlement move closer together into a well-knit union. Together with this kind of union social relationships and the rights and responsibilities that go with them increase and even potentize. Living together in such a village requires a far greater measure of care, regard and renunciation of individual interests and tribal or family individualism than elsewhere.

5)   The surprising result was this:
town (enclosure, fence, manor, village):
1. Dial. Any cluster of houses recognized as a distinct place; a village.
2. a) A center of population, larger and more fully organized than a village, but not incorporated.
b) Eng. as a city. A village with a periodical fair or market; more fully *market town.*
c) Any large closely populated place, as a city, borough or an urban district.
This was not really found to be helpful. A look into the meaning of the word *city* yielded little more:
1. Any important town.
2. Brit. A town traditionally entitled city, usually one that has been an episcopal see.
3. U.S. A muncipal corporation occupying a definite area and subject to the state from which it derives its powers.
Webster's New Collegiate Dictionary, 1953.

6)   Bader, *Village-Association and Village-Congregation* p. 195-6.

7)   Bader, *Village-Association and Village-Congregation* p. 199-200.

8)   *Das unauffindbare Dorf.* Unvereinbare Zielsetzungen, Wünsche im Widerspruch. Leszek Kolakowski, 1980, Lausanne, Switzerland.

9)   The following excellent book contains many descriptions and pictures relevant to this essay. For instance:
"There is a drawing of the circular plan of a village in Brazil — a compound of the Bororo Indians in the Mato Grosso region, showing the complex dual organization into clan houses radiating from a central men's house. Missionaries realized that the most permanent way of converting these people was to make them abandon their concentrically balanced villages and relocate them in houses set in parallel rows."
The Houses of Mankind, Colin Duly/Thames and Hudson Blacker, Calmann Cooper, Ltd. 1979.
How many societal phenomena have been ascribed erroneously to quite different causes than those entailing placing houses in rows! Gradually, certain social entities began to crumble and explanations for this were sought in all kinds of directions. People became susceptible to conversion to all manner of persuasions. All the while, houses were increasingly placed along roads and streets in bands. Are we to speak here of the great city developments, of the pigeon-hole concept for providing places to sleep, to be and to work? The as yet unbroken might of these 'projects' ingests thousands and hundreds of thousands of people, making them leave land and field and inherited skills to settle in squalid boxes of misery and deprivation in slums and ghettos.

10)   One of the first children's villages was undertaken in the name of Pestalozzi in Switzerland. And there were, of course, the many, many S.O.S. children's villages. They all had something moving and enthusing to them. In 1946 the foundation stone to the Pestalozzi village was laid. At this occasion a school girl from the large village of Trogen nearby which sponsored this children's extension, called out four times into the four directions of the world: "You girls and boys, who have neither father nor mother, you can come to us. Your room is ready." As it had been in the villages of old, the concern of the community turned to the acceptance of the poor, the sick and the orphaned as their solemn duty. This often went parallel to the establishment of a school, a schoolhouse, or at least the appointment of a school master.
A remarkable contribution to the subject appeared in "Du", Periodical for Art and Culture 8/1984. Zürich. The actual words in Swiss-German were: "Ihr Maetle ond Buebe, wo kaen Vater und kae Muetter meh hend, choend zu ues ue, d'Stobe isch parat."

11)   The older village communities regarded the office of the shepherd hardly less important than the forester, or game and hunting master. This office reaches, of course, far beyond the start of village communities. Day-and-night-shepherds existed, but also cow and horse shepherds, and pig and sheep shepherds. [In fact the pig shepherd was especially honored in ancient Greece as his office was inherited and a certain amount of prophecy and clairvoyance often went with it.]
"As a rule the community appointed only a single shepherd who was to bother himself to find helpers and who was responsible for them." Bader, p. 318e.
For a detailed and engaging description of shepherds, see Roumeli, *Travels in Northern Greece*, Patrick Leigh *Fermor*, Penguin Travel Library. Penguin Books Ltd., Harmondsworth, Middlesex, England 1966/1983/1985; p.48.

12)   These and many other such brotherly conversations are embedded in a larger village life of which only a few superscriptions can be given here. To these belong: the Bible Evening; the Services; the College meetings, during which a deeper image of a child and its special circumstance and need is evoked; the four-year Seminar in Curative/Special Education; the annual courses in Social Therapy; the festivals with their music, much of it composed in the villages; with their plays and their many other offerings; the choirs; the visits by well-known artists, chiefly musicians; the open-house days and the workshops with parents; the annual days of earnest discussions with the siblings of the exceptional individuals; the exhibitions of craftwork, and the talks to parents, the public and at professional gatherings. It is a panorama of activities arising from the chosen task of these villages spoken of above. The villages' origins, their response and their goals belong to the future out of which a call reaches, now and then, to some who hear....

PHOTO INDEX